simpleSolutions

Patios and Decks

simpleSolutions

Patios and Decks

COLEEN CAHILL

Foreword by Timothy Drew
Managing Editor, *Home Magazine*

FRIEDMAN/FAIRFAX

A FRIEDMAN/FAIRFAX BOOK

© 2002 by Michael Friedman Publishing Group, Inc.

Please visit our website: www.metrobooks.com

Cahill, Coleen.
    Patios and decks / Coleen Cahill; foreword by Timothy Drew.
        p. cm. – (SimpleSolutions)
    Includes bibliographical references (p.).
    ISBN 1-58663-164-0
    1. Patios. 2. Decks (Architecture, Domestic) 3. Garden ornaments and furniture.
    I. Title. II. Series.

    NA8375 .C35 2002
    747.7'9—dc21

                                                                    2001040711

EDITOR: Rosy Ngo
ART DIRECTOR: Jeff Batzli
DESIGNER: Midori Nakamura
PHOTO EDITOR: Paquita Bass
PRODUCTION MANAGER: Richela Fabian Morgan

Color separations by Fine Arts Repro House Co., Ltd.
Printed in China by C & C Offset Printing Co., Ltd.

10 9 8 7 6 5 4 3 2 1

Distributed by Sterling Publishing Company, Inc.
387 Park Avenue South
New York, NY 10016
Distributed in Canada by Sterling Publishing
Canadian Manda Group
One Atlantic Avenue, Suite 105
Toronto, Ontario, Canada M6K 3E7
Distributed in Australia by
Capricorn Link (Australia) Pty Ltd.
P.O. Box 704
Windsor, NSW 2756, Australia

Acknowledgments

Thank you to Tim Drew from *Home Magazine* for contributing the foreword, and to Paquita Bass, Lori Epstein, Kate Perry, and Rosy Ngo from Friedman/Fairfax. Special thanks to Sharyn Rosart.

Contents

Foreword

Once upon a time, there was an inside and there was an outside, and no one thought much about it. However, that was, thankfully, a long, long time ago. People have since come to relish those in-between spaces, those that share elements of both the indoors and the outdoors. While the concepts of patios and decks are not new ones, it's probably safe to say that in recent years, they've evolved to become quite sophisticated spaces. Like so many aspects of the way we live, we've taken inspiration from a wide variety of sources rooted in a number of different cultures. An import from Mexico, the patio—a word adopted into English in 1828—is a prime example. Without stretching too far back into history, we might guess that the atrium of the ancient Roman house was also part of the evolution.

Speaking of evolution, there was a time when "patio" was a rather pretentious name for a mere patch of concrete or flagstones furnished with a picnic table and a rusty barbecue grill. Elementary as these early versions may have been, those of us who grew up with them have cherished memories of family and friends gathered for holiday cookouts. Clearly, where you grew up made a big difference as to what you thought a patio was.

Decks and patios have become virtual outdoor rooms that are equipped, furnished, and outfitted with an incredible number of comforts and amenities— everything from elaborate cooking facilities (the quick-rusting barbecue grill from the hardware store having gone the way of the dinosaur) to hot tubs, lap pools, and gurgling fountains, not to mention breath-taking plantings.

These open-air rooms can be anything you want them to be. And deciding what you want them to be is the very first task to accomplish in planning a deck or patio. As you look through the pages of this book, the stunning collection of wonderful photographs will likely first grab your attention. You'll find elegant retreats, slick outdoor havens, and homey hideaways. Some are expansive spaces designed for year-round use in sunny climates; others are more intimate, ready to offer serene moments while enjoying the season's pleasures. The key is to select the elements that will work for you and your family—and, of course, your climate. What's feasible in Southern California or Florida may not be workable in Wisconsin. An open-air kitchen might be just the thing in Santa Barbara, but it would likely take a beating during a Minneapolis winter. However, no one says that a Minnesotan can't have the main kitchen opening out onto an adjacent outdoor dining area. There are solutions—it's all a matter of adapting and combining your favorite ideas to your personal needs. That's what this book is about. There's grand inspiration and a vast array of tips and pointers that will get you well on your way to the pleasures of the open air that you're looking for.

Lastly, once you have your deck or patio just the way you want it, remember to enjoy it. Relish the warm breezes, listen to the wind in the trees, look at the stars in the night sky. Savor the quiet times with your partner and children, and have a great time at your summer bashes. Watch the sunset, and wait for the fireflies to come out.

Timothy Drew
Managing Editor, *Home Magazine*

Introduction

One of the most enjoyable ways to expand your home and life into the outdoors is with a deck or patio that provides a space to relax, entertain, or simply take pleasure in being outside. Entertaining has always been popular, and many of today's decks and patios include full kitchens that can turn out multicourse meals. And for some, an outdoor space serves as a retreat from the hectic world, offering a private place to unwind and enjoy amenities like hot tubs and lap pools.

There are many different ideas about the elements that make up the perfect outdoor space, but the ideal space for you will be the one that works with your home and reflects the way you live. Sift through your memories for images of the perfect summer afternoon, and meld them with the ways you and your family like to spend time outdoors. That's the best way to ensure that your outdoor space suits your needs and captures your dreams.

In warm-weather climates, the outdoors is an integral part of daily life. Decks and patios allow easy movement between indoors and out. Not only a popular way of expanding "square footage," a deck or patio may increase the perceived value of your home. And when an outdoor space is incorporated into its overall design, the result is an integrated solution that expands the functionality of the home and enhances its enjoyment by the whole family.

In northern climates, the brevity of the summer season may dictate some of the choices made for an outdoor space. Still, the pleasure of having a deck or patio may be that much more intense when you know that cold weather is just around the corner.

Decks are the most popular and cost-effective way to add an outdoor space to your home. A traditional wood deck, built off the back of the house, is standard on many newly constructed homes. Most of these decks are built with treated lumber, while natural woods like cedar and redwood offer a more expensive—and beautiful—alternative. Composite woods are a new material growing in popularity. Budget will likely be an important factor in determining the right material for your deck.

Whether you enjoy a magnificent view of the ocean or a simple backyard scene, factor a deck into your house plans. For someone who enjoys do-it-yourself projects, building a deck might be just the summer challenge needed. If you're not particularly handy, nor is anyone in your family, then call in professionals. They can help you design a deck that suits your home and meets your personal tastes and needs. (Plus, a professional can do the work of making sure the deck is structurally sound and meets all building codes—steps you'd have to take if building your own.) Keep in mind that it's never too late to think about a deck—it's an easy addition to an existing home.

Constructing a patio is a bit more complicated than building a deck, and it's best to consult a professional. Once you've decided on a location, a professional will tackle issues like drainage, leveling the ground, and removing excess dirt. And his or her skills are essential when it comes time to lay the actual patio.

Patios are slightly more versatile than decks in that they come in all different shapes and can feature a wide range of materials—from standard brick to natural stone. Another benefit of a patio is that it can be located away from the house—positioned to make the most of the afternoon sun, for example, or tucked away in a corner of the yard for a bit of privacy. Freestanding patios can also be designed to blend in with natural surroundings, and often make use of some of nature's landmarks. A large tree or stone can be incorporated right into the layout of a patio, while a nearby stream may define its outer edge. Consider using local stone for a retreat that truly blends in with its environment.

When planning an outdoor space, it's important to consider the look of your home. The architectural style of the house—whether Victorian or modern—will

help determine the design of the deck or patio. This area should take its cues from the details and materials used in the home, as well as respect its scale. A contemporary home requires a sleek design solution, while a cozy cottage may be best paired with a small patio.

The chosen plot of land is also an important factor when planning an outdoor area—both its size and contours will come into play. A house on a steeply sloped site or one surrounded by woods may require a different solution than a beach house with an open stretch to the ocean. Tailoring the deck or patio space to a specific plot of land will ensure its stability and help to integrate it into the natural landscape.

Keep in mind that no space is too small for a pleasant open-air retreat. Remember that where there is a will, there is a way—city gardeners around the world are proof of that. Small balconies and rooftops are frequently transformed into oases of green by intrepid urban gardeners with a love of plants and the outdoors.

Consider the design elements of your home and the surrounding landscape, while keeping in mind the limitations of space and budget, and you'll be well on your way to creating your ideal out-of-doors environment. Whether that's an expansive patio with the latest barbecue equipment or a tidy deck that overlooks the garden beneath a vine-covered pergola, simpleSolutions: *Patios and Decks* can provide the inspiration you need. Filled with ideas that will help you see the potential of your own home, and tips for making your dream patio or deck a reality, it's the ideal companion as you journey into the outdoors!

Coleen Cahill

Indoor-Outdoor Transitions

Blending the architectural styles of indoor and outdoor spaces makes great design sense. If you're building a new home, consider bringing together professionals—architect, landscape designer, builder—to share ideas and troubleshoot. If you are adding an outdoor living space to an existing house, take your design cues from the style of your home. Look at its boldest features—roofline, materials, colors, windows—and integrate the most appealing elements of the architecture into your outdoor environment.

This home was designed to maximize enjoyment of the out-of-doors and capitalize on the panoramic view. Glass walls slide out of the way, virtually eliminating the barrier between interior and exterior. The wraparound deck is partially covered by the building's overhang, and the solid wall that surrounds it ensures that it feels like an integral part of the house's design. ➲

A contemporary home calls for a deck with strong geometric shapes. This open deck is integrated seamlessly into the design of the home, allowing guests and regular traffic to flow easily between the indoor and outdoor areas. Stairs from a terrace off the kitchen and from the main living room lead down to the deck, while a third set of steps provides access to the yard below. ☊

A modern courtyard features an elongated pool that reflects the neat proportions of the house. The roof of the house has been extended to create a shady sitting area along the length of the facade. Wraparound decking also unifies the outdoor area. Wide steps lead down to the pool, while a handsome pergola draws the eye upward, bridging the pool and visually uniting the indoor and outdoor architecture. ↻

Perching at the edge of the pool, this patio functions as a man-made beach. Although shallow in depth, this area runs nearly the entire length of the home, providing plenty of space to accommodate a series of chaises for swimmers in need of a rest. The simple furnishings and unadorned look are in keeping with the strong lines of the home's architecture. ⚓

Chunky columns and an overhead structure painted to blend with the roof define an outdoor walkway.

Sleek and streamlined, this modern ranch home yields effortlessly to a partially covered deck, which then opens to a pool. The sitting area is shaded by a slatted roof that adds to the clean lines of the home. The result is—literally—an outdoor room. Beyond, a series of wide steps leads to the lawn and the pool. ◖

A lakeside home nestles into the woods with a spacious side deck. This very simple design complements the architecture of the home while blending beautifully into the natural surroundings. An existing tree was cleverly accommodated and now stands as the centerpiece for circular bench seating, while the freestanding furniture in bent willow adds to the woodsy feel. ↻

Note the massive logs that serve as supports for the deck, further linking the cabin and outdoor areas together.

S et on the banks of a fast-moving stream, this rustic log cabin makes the most of its dramatic surroundings. Several interconnected decks, designed to take advantage of the view on all sides, encircle the home. By featuring wood in the same warm tones as the logs used for the cabin, the deck becomes a natural extension of the home, seamlessly integrating the overall design into the environment. ➲

Taking in the View

Whether a home overlooks the ocean, a cityscape, or a well-tended private garden, its outdoor "room" should be positioned to take full advantage of the view. If the view is **panoramic**, a spacious deck running the length of the house may afford the greatest **enjoyment** of the vista, while smaller terraces, patios, and landings can be designed to capture a more focused scene. Careful planning is the key to ensuring that an exterior space makes the most of its setting. Don't forget to think about **exposure** to natural elements like sun and wind, and how they might affect your use of an outdoor area.

bright ideas

▶ Extend a section of the deck as far as possible to maximize views

▶ Install retractable awnings that offer protection without closing in the space

▶ Use lower-profile railings and balustrades

This beach house features double doors in the living room that open onto a small deck with unobstructed views of the ocean. The deck is very basic in its construction, eschewing railings or other details that might obscure the view. A step leads down from the deck to a stone patio. Sturdy chaises invite repose. ♋

Tucked into a corner at one side of the home, a stone patio feels like an outdoor living room with the open water just steps away. Enclosed by low stone walls on two sides, the compact space makes a cozy sitting area when outfitted with solid wood furnishings sporting plush cushions. The patio continues along the front of the house, offering a subtle invitation into this intimate gathering area. ☊

The dramatic setting of this home was the inspiration for its wraparound deck. To create an outdoor area that would provide both shade and shelter from the wind, some indoor square footage on the ground floor was sacrificed, allowing the second story overhang to create a roof for part of the deck. Construction of the deck was kept deliberately simple, with a single, low railing encircling it for safety, ensuring that the view of the water remains the main attraction. ◔

Sometimes less is more: a spare, serene deck lets the spectacular ocean view dominate. This simple yet spacious deck features both a covered section that provides shelter from the midday sun and an open area that allows for full exposure. Details and clutter are kept to a minimum, and furnishings can be moved as needed. ◑

This cheerful deck is perfectly positioned to take advantage of the woodsy surroundings and water view. Two pop-outs extend the deck surface and add visual interest, while the white railing, topped with finials, complements the trim on this traditional home. ↻

The shingles featured on the house are reprised on the deck walls and support structure.

Crisp and contemporary in attitude, this townhouse sports a sleek deck overlooking the active harbor. Modern touches include the deck's red metal rails, wire chairs, and a glass occasional table. The overall effect is that of a cheerful perch ideal for entertaining a small circle of friends. ➲

A pair of lamps illuminates the deck at night, when the lights of the harbor offer a sparkling view.

A Spot to Sit

ssential to the enjoyment of outdoor space is a comfortable spot in which to **sit and relax.** Just as you would curl up indoors in a favorite overstuffed chair, you can relax outdoors as well if you create a similar **cozy corner.** A couple of chairs encourage quiet conversation; seating for one offers the possibility of a private moment away from the main activity. If you're designing a new deck, think about incorporating built-in seating. Either way, fix a tall glass of iced tea and find a spot to sit!

bright ideas

▶ Apply plastic protectors to chair legs so they can be moved easily and without marring the surface

▶ Cover furniture with fade- and mildew-resistant fabrics for protection from the weather

▶ Add an old-fashioned touch with rockers, swings, and gliders

Relaxing in such a setting—complete with a pair of lounge chairs featuring stretched canvas seats—is as close to paradise as one can expect to get. The stone floor provides a cool respite for bare feet, while the bamboo shades offer protection from the tropical sun as well as a passing shower. A soothing grass and brick path leads to a second patio space off the pool. ⏻

A rugged Adirondack chair and side table suit the rustic nature of this mountain retreat, and have been moved to a quiet corner of the deck to invite contemplative moments. The exposed beams on the ceiling above echo both the lines of the chair and its natural wood coloring. ↻

A lightweight wicker chair and table can be easily carried inside at the end of the day or if the weather turns gloomy.

Sliding doors open onto a stone patio perfect for an afternoon of reading and relaxing. The main deck is around the corner, so this spot offers a bit of seclusion. A stone wall encircles the patio, and is low enough to allow the view to be fully enjoyed. The wall's gentle curve reflects the shape and contour of the landscape beyond. ◑

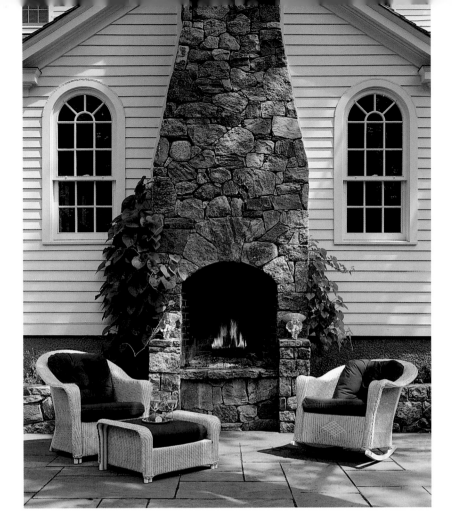

An outdoor fireplace is the focal point of this patio, and make it the natural place to create a cozy seating area. The wicker chair, ottoman, and rocker are classic choices that reflect the traditional style of the home, while the comfortable cushions are covered in a solid, durable fabric. The warmth of the open flame allows this patio to be enjoyed well beyond summer—turning it into a multiseason outdoor space. ☞

Clear panels encircling this sun-bleached deck offer protection from the ocean's spray without obscuring the stunning view. Because of this nontraditional "railing," the intricately carved demi-chaise with cane seating can face the pounding surf unobstructed. The weathered decking and warm tones of the chaise offer an interesting contrast. ➲

Permanent seating should be situated where it takes best advantage of the surroundings. This tiled patio features benches with a dual purpose: they serve as a border for the flowerbed and present a convenient place to rest and enjoy the garden. The colorful benches are works of art, featuring hand-painted ceramic tiles surrounded by a mosaic of broken tile pieces. ➲

Lightweight furniture or pieces on rolling casters can be shifted to the optimum spot to enjoy the surroundings—even as those surroundings change with the seasons and the time of day. Here, a weathered Adirondack chair has been drawn up to the edge of a sun-bleached deck to take advantage of the ocean breeze and the view of the rolling dunes. ➲

The traditional garden bench is a classic seating option. This one has an intricately patterned back, and is nestled amid the plantings on a brick patio, creating an inviting place to sit and admire the greenery. ➲

An aged wooden half barrel, filled with ornamental grasses that reflect the terrain, anchors the corner of the deck.

Organic Shapes

ight angles are not necessarily suitable for every space. If you are designing a deck or patio, take the opportunity to think about a more **organic** shape. Constructing a deck or patio with **curves** can offset the angularity of a house, helping to integrate the structure into the **natural contours** of the terrain. A good choice for a small or unusually shaped area, curves can highlight a particular view or create a more secluded spot.

bright ideas

▶ Create an instant conversation area with built-in benches along a curved edge

▶ Use round or oval garden tables to complement organic shapes

▶ Build curved steps to offset an angular deck

Wrapping around the house, this deck creates a variety of vantage points for full enjoyment of the lake view, while the circular seating area promotes sociability. In this charming rounded corner, the decking has been laid in a circular pattern to set the area apart from the rest of the deck.

The landscape around this shapely deck—sloping woods with a meandering stream—is reflected in its design. The floating, curvaceous deck is a series of arcs and ovals, a structure truly in harmony with its environment. The main seating area is a large, open oval that extends over the creek while embracing guests with its roomy built-in bench. ☚

Large trees on the site have been worked into the deck's design, infusing the space with a feeling of the forest.

The gentle arc of this redwood deck extends gracefully into the backyard, increasing the surface area of the deck and creating a more interesting silhouette. Its porch-inspired design features a curved brick foundation, painted white to match the house; posts that recall square columns with decorative moldings on the top and bottom; shaped handrails; and painted balusters. ☚

P oised to enjoy the magnificent water view from any vantage point, this split-level deck features undulating curves that offset its linear dimensions. Extending the rounded steps along the length of the house adds visual interest and creates several distinct areas within the deck. ↻

plan ahead

- ☐ Identify trees and other aspects of the landscape that call for an organic solution
- ☐ Mimic the contours of a round pool, or design an undulating deck to offset a rectangular pool
- ☐ Bring panache to pathways by adding curves and turns—the most direct route may not be the most scenic

Note the glass panels beneath the railing that protect against the wind.

On a Different Level

A steeply sloped site can present a major challenge when designing a deck. The solution is often a **multilevel** structure that incorporates the incline of the land into its design. A deck with different levels has **practical** advantages, too. Individual platforms can be reserved for specific activities such as cooking, dining, and relaxing. For extra design interest, consider changing the direction of the boards on each level, or incorporate built-in benches and planters to further **define areas**.

bright ideas

▶ Create zones designated for specific activities: cooking, eating, sunbathing

▶ Incorporate a permanent shade structure on one level

▶ Differentiate levels with materials, direction of boards, color

▶ Light stairs for safety

A three-tiered deck set on an evergreen-studded slope flows down toward the water's edge. The area closest to the house provides the best views and is spacious enough for entertaining, while more informal meals can take place on the middle level. The lowest level is ideal for stargazing or wildlife-watching. Weathered planks and a straightforward design are in keeping with the rustic setting, proving that the simplest deck is sometimes the best solution.

So seamless is the transition between this house and deck that it is difficult to tell where one ends and the other begins. The warm, varnished wood of the deck makes it feel like a natural extension of the home, and creates a unified look that blends in with the surrounding woods. The narrow platform adjacent to the house provides a transition, while the larger deck unfolds a few steps below. ↻

A simple railing runs around all the decked levels, providing a unifying element.

Red(wood), white, and blue provide the decorative theme for this classic deck. White risers and boards laid in different directions distinguish the two levels. Traditional posts and balusters complement the white trim found on the house and the overhang, which provides a shaded area on the top level of the deck. Classic white wicker furnishings complete the picture. ➲

Multiple levels and mini-walls create a series of attractive yet functional areas to accommodate a large family that enjoys spending time outdoors. Angling down from the house, the main area includes a table and chairs for summer meals; jutting out to one side is a lower level for playing or sunbathing. Plenty of room allows just enough separation to keep everyone happy. ◖

Brushed stainless steel rails are combined with redwood for a sleek look that extends to all the levels.

On this spectacular deck, different levels are devoted to specific functions, defining the space more like traditional interiors. The focal point is the "conversation pit," which features a built-in, multi-sided bench that can easily accommodate a large group; a fire pit at its center creates an outdoor hearth— a luxurious "campfire" indeed. ☾

Set apart for privacy and shaded by a pergola, the spa commands the upper deck level.

Just outside the French doors, two handsome chairs offer a relaxing spot for a quiet moment—overlooking, but not too close to, the conversation area. ☊

Shade and Shelter

rchitectural structures, whether incorporated into the deck or patio or situated separately, add style as well as function. Options range from simple **trellises** designed for coaxing vines skyward to elaborate **gazebos** with soaring rooflines and built-in seating. Styles vary from nostalgic and charming to spare and modern. Think about which type of architectural element will suit your space, and whether you want a completely enclosed outdoor "room" or just a shady shelter. Either way, you'll be upping the style quotient of your deck or patio.

bright ideas

▶ Suspend chairs from the beams of a pergola for whimsical seating

▶ Fashion a pest-free outdoor dining room by screening in a gazebo

▶ Mark entrances with arbors (then encourage climbing vines)

Custom-built benches blend with the decking.

A Zen-like peace pervades this spacious deck, which harbors a small but enchanting pavilion in one corner. Painted to match the softly weathered wood of the deck, the pavilion introduces a vertical element and raises the eye above a single plane. The roof shelters any visitors to this serene space from the elements, while a tree incorporated into the deck anchors the corner opposite.

This charming if somewhat unorthodox gazebo is a graceful addition to a beautifully landscaped yard. Set just off the patio's edge, it is both an integral part of the space and at a slight remove. The gazebo's gently arched windows and conical roof make a strong architectural statement, while glass windows provide an extra measure of protection against inclement weather and turn the gazebo into more than just a summertime retreat. ☾

The decking was sealed with a clear finish to showcase the natural color of the redwood, while the railings and trim were painted white for contrast.

Images of a bygone era spring to mind at the sight of this nostalgic, white-trimmed gazebo with its classic weathervane. Built upon a small hill, it takes advantage of the gently rolling terrain, and gives the deck a Victorian charm. ☊

Wooden slats cover a deck that leads to a separate home office. Although the deck is protected from direct sunlight, light and air can flow freely through the overhead structure. Situated between the main part of the home and the office, this area can serve as an adjunct to either, with the large table in the center acting as a desk or a spot to eat and entertain. ↻

If you are building a deck, think about incorporating a sheltered area. This deck, which wraps around the house, was built high above the ground to enjoy lots of light—but a special corner was reserved for a gazebo-style cover. Slender posts support the roof so as not to interfere with the expansive view. ➲

This handsome pergola, which extends directly from the side of the house, adds a classic architectural element to the traditional shingle-style home—and is a beautiful marriage of form and function. The crisp white woodwork complements the trim on the house, and is sturdy enough to support the heaviest of vines, such as grape and wisteria. ↻

The pergola's slats are far enough apart to allow a wealth of sunlight to warm the slate patio beneath. At the center of the patio is a custom-built circular table with three perfect arcs for benches. The circular shapes complement the cylindrical columns and balusters that surround the patio. ➲

Built-In Convenience

uilt-in or custom-built units for seating, planting, or storage are versatile choices for expanding the functionality and efficiency of your outdoor space. To get started, think about what types of activities you and your family plan to do outside. Then prepare a list of all the features you would like included in the deck plans. Don't forget to consider the details of your location, including the natural features such as trees, and the amount of exposure to the elements.

Built-in benches can be transformed into comfortable seating simply by adding cushions and pillows. Here, a collection of throw pillows in bold stripes and summery cobalt turn a weathered bench into a convenient place to rest before or after meals. The table can even be drawn up to the bench to provide extra seating. ♫

In this case, the tree came first. A huge, old oak makes a wonderful focal point for this deck. The owners decided not only to incorporate it into their plans, but to make the tree (and the shade it offered) central to the deck by encircling it with a wide bench. Now that's turning a problem into a solution! 🎧

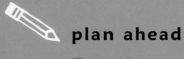

plan ahead

- ☐ Consider an in-ground sprinkler system for efficient watering of plants
- ☐ Ensure that bare wood surfaces of built-in seating are splinter-free by using sandpaper
- ☐ Think about built-in storage when planning an outdoor kitchen

The owners of this home had entertaining in mind when they designed this conversation area featuring a fire pit. There's plenty of room on the built-in, semicircular bench, and even cool evenings can be enjoyed out-of-doors around the open flame. ☻

D on't overlook storage when planning your outdoor space. Custom storage lets you keep frequently used items nearby, and makes cleanup a cinch. This redwood bench has a hinged top, which opens to reveal ample storage space. ➲

P lanters edging the tiers of this deck are both decorative and functional: the marigolds and petunias add a vivid splash of color, while the boxes frame the deck's edges. ➾

Patio Pleasures

 A more intimately scaled yard often calls for a patio rather than a deck. The three most important considerations when planning a patio are **site, size, and shape.** The location and exposure of a patio will dictate how and when it is used. The size depends on how much of the yard you want to take over and the features you want on the patio. Straight lines will maximize the space, but curvy shapes are sometimes more pleasing to the eye. Once you've addressed the three Ss, it's time to focus on the details: paving options, seating plans, plants, and any other amenities that will create the patio of your dreams.

bright ideas

▶ Create patterns with pavers: herringbone, basket weave, etc.

▶ Use potted plants to mark the edges of a patio

▶ Add an outdoor fireplace to enjoy year-round

Tucked under the eaves of a wood-and-stone house, this patio is linked by its design to both the surrounding landscape and the house. The irregularly cut stone is complemented by an edging of boulders, while the furnishings echo the home's crisp white trim.

With country charm to spare, this simple patio melds harmoniously with an old stone house. The square stones give the patio a tidy, compact air, but there is plenty of room for a small table surrounded by handsome chairs and garden benches. ➲

Brick is the most popular choice for attractive, long-lasting patios. Even after years of exposure to weather and use, brick maintains its character and earthy appeal. Here, a detached brick patio surrounded by greenery serves as a delightful setting for a summer lunch. ➴

Local stone was used to create a naturalistic patio with undefined boundaries just outside this cozy cottage. A collection of white Adirondack chairs and a bench painted to match the house create an informal spot for dining or simply relaxing outdoors. ☻

Use what nature offers: here, a tree stump has been turned into the base of a small table!

Creative paving options abound. For instance, tiles of different sizes can be used like mosaic pieces, laid in curving or angular patterns. The unexpected choice is often the key to distinctive style—here, colored insets add whimsical flair. ➲

Get curvy with patio edges: an undulating border adds visual interest to a patio or pathway.

Brick, stone, iron, and wood are the enduring elements of this small but charming outdoor dining room. The formal stone dining table, which rests on curvy columns, is surrounded by traditional garden dining chairs with lattice-style backs. An iron fence creates a border. ◖

A large patio constructed of brick laid in a basket-weave pattern has been zoned into distinct yet connected areas. Slate borders and distinct furniture groupings help to define each space. ↻

Don't let a small space deter you: it may be the perfect location for a petite patio. Here, French doors open onto an intimate oasis of tropical plants and trees. The sinuous wrought-iron furnishings are simply adorned with white cushions that can be easily removed; a collection of potted plants adds to the lushness. ☮

A patio can be used to draw together different areas of the home. Here an L-shaped house features a patio that feels like a courtyard, uniting the two separate wings. Large pieces of slate have been laid in a harmonious design to create the patio's surface, and the slate is reprised on the fireplace hearth and wide ledges atop the walls of raised beds. ◑

Private Time

When you are ready to **escape** the hectic world, step out onto your private deck or patio and find true relaxation. There are many attractive ways to achieve privacy outdoors. First, consider whether you'd like to **enclose** your entire outdoor space or select one area to be private and leave the rest open. Shrubs and trees create living barriers to sight and noise. Fences, screens, and other structures offer instant **privacy**, and a measure of security, too.

bright ideas

▶ Match the design (and/or color) of fencing to the architectural style of the house

▶ Incorporate a solid fence topped with lattice to provide a measure of privacy without the closed-in feeling of a high fence

▶ Place screens strategically to create intimate spaces within the patio

Plants combine beautifully with fences—the greenery softens the fencing's strict lines, and layering of plants and fencing enhances privacy.

Lattice is a classic choice for privacy—and it conveys old-fashioned garden charm. This delightful patio is enclosed on two sides by lattice walls adorned with large Versailles boxes brimming with impatiens. Architectural columns enhance the classical feel, and encourage vines and climbers.

Especially in urban settings, where space can be limited and privacy hard to find, a wall is often the best way to create a peaceful retreat. Here, a high brick wall has been adorned with a small fountain and decorative garden objects. Vines add a touch of green and soften the effect of solid brick. An umbrella shields visitors from too much sun—and from the view of those in surrounding buildings.

This modern, cement-faced home required an architecturally appropriate privacy solution. A cement wall with a large cut-out "window" looks out on the garden beyond, while letting additional light and air into the patio area. A pair of curvy woven chairs completes the modern look. ➲

A pergola provides some shade for the bench and supports hanging plants.

Redwood screens in two different designs make a striking statement. The solid fence faces the property line and provides complete privacy, while the open screen shields without inhibiting the flow of air and light. Built-in benches accommodate guests and echo the geometric look of the structures. ⊂

Poolside

iving into a **cool** pool on a hot summer day is one of life's greatest pleasures—even the idea of water brings a sense of **relief**. The rectangular turquoise pool that may spring to mind, however, is a thing of the past; today's pools make unique design statements. In landscape terms, the pool and the deck or patio that surround it are of one piece—a cohesive motif is **essential**. There are also numerous practical and safety considerations; if you are planning a pool, professional assistance is a must.

bright ideas

▶ Note that fencing around pools provides safety and is sometimes required by law

▶ Create a snack center near the pool to minimize trips in and out of the house

▶ Score and tint concrete to look like terra-cotta tiles

A gently curved redwood deck surrounds this black-bottomed lap pool, which features brick coping. An existing oak tree was incorporated into the deck, lending shade and a leafy pool reflection. ➲

*A small bridge leads to
the covered hot tub area.*

Set on a wooded lot, this stunning
contemporary home uses expanses of glass
to erase the boundary between indoors and
out. A minimal aesthetic highlights natural
textures and materials. The long, narrow
lap pool is set into a long, narrow deck of
weathered cedar, which is edged with rocks.
A covered walkway, illuminated at ground
level, adds a meditative quality. ☊

A Mediterranean mood prevails around this luxurious pool. Warm terra-cotta tiles form a two-level patio surrounding the pool, with a ceramic tile wall separating the upper and lower levels. Varying shades of blue provide cooling contrast: the deep cerulean of the pool is echoed in the navy tiles of the half-wall and the blue-and-white patterns of the pool tiles and stair risers. ↻

Floating "islands" provide a perch for potted pansies that add a splash of color to the pool.

Custom pools create the opportunity for truly inspired designs. In this example, two distinct sections of a pool make a single design statement. Echoing the contours of the house, the gentle curve of one section of the pool is a pleasing counterpoint to the angularity of the rest of the house and pool walls. ➲

Brick, wood, and aggregate stone make an appealing trio for a patio and deck combination in a spectacular setting. The narrow, undulating pool has a brick coping paired with an aggregate flooring that extends to the point where a table and chairs are positioned to admire the view. A simple redwood deck flows down from the house to the edge of the pool, then right over it with a small bridge. ↻

Strategically positioned potted plants mark the edges of the deck.

Good design integrates the pool into the natural beauty of its setting. The pool almost disappears into the vast expanse of wooden decking. Simple furnishings, plus a few potted plants, minimize the intrusion of the man-made into this serene landscape. ➲

Outdoor Spas

An outdoor spa, alone or in conjunction with a swimming pool, can be the relaxing centerpiece of a **backyard haven**. Practical considerations are similar to those for a pool area (most important is a water- and slip-resistant surface). You'll also want to think about privacy, shade, and nighttime lighting. Then it's time for **a long soak!**

bright ideas

▶ Add a nearby relaxation area with comfortable chairs

▶ Consider wiring the spa area with stereo speakers

▶ Create subtle lighting with colored gels for nighttime soaks

The centerpiece of this redwood deck is a swim-in-place Jacuzzi-jet pool that sits atop a raised platform partially sheltered by an elaborate pergola. The soaring pavilion is the focal point of the spa area, drawing the eye upward with dramatic arches and lattice accents. Below, on either side of the pool, built-in benches with rounded backs and lattice inserts echo the design of the pavilion. ♙

Privacy abounds here, with the surrounding leafy trees offering a natural screen. Steps on the left and right side of the above-ground Jacuzzi offer multiple entry areas. Extra-wide crosspieces serve as a handy ledge for placing wine glasses and candles out of the whirlpool's spray. ☯

This expansive redwood deck invites relaxation and sociability, with an ample hot tub set next to a circular conversation pit. A series of gently rising steps leads to the upper deck, where the tub is sheltered by an Eastern-inspired pergola (note also the decorative wooden "window" set into the privacy screen). ↻

A cozy corner surrounded by palms is the perfect location for this tempting spa. The mosaic design—reminiscent of Roman baths—adds to the leafy motif. The luxuriant foliage, along with the seclusion of a corner site, creates a private oasis for supremely indulgent relaxation. ➲

Hooks make towels easily accessible.

A Mediterranean-style home extends the theme to an expansive patio, with bright white and warm clay tones providing the backdrop for a deep blue swimming pool and adjacent built-in whirlpool tub. Chunky angles abound, from the stairs leading down to the pool, to the bookend-like pedestals. A single type of brick is used extensively throughout the patio, echoing the home's clay roof tiles and drawing the designs together. ◑

Plenty of open space around a pool leaves room to move about freely.

Lush vegetation frames this pool-tub combination. Asymmetrical shapes make the most of the space, and are visually appealing in themselves. Setting the tub and pool in close proximity makes it easy to move between the two. ➲

Cooking Alfresco

he backyard barbecue is practically a summertime institution. Food cooked over an **open flame** is irresistible to most of us, and in the last decade, outdoor cooking equipment has begun to rival its indoor counterparts. Whether you're planning to invest in the latest **high-tech** grill or prefer the slow-burning character of charcoal briquettes, creating an open-air "kitchen" should be part of your plans. If you have a lot of space to work with, think about what you would like in a **fully equipped** outdoor cooking area. Remember, however, that no deck or patio is too small for a cookout center—careful planning and a few simple solutions can make all the difference—so get ready to grill!

bright ideas

- Plan ahead for gas, electrical, and plumbing needs
- Extend countertops to accommodate bar stools
- Choose a full-size sink instead of a bar sink for greater capacity and convenience

This outdoor kitchen was designed with serious cooking in mind. At its center is a brick hearth, flanked by ample tiled countertops. Warm meals are prepared on the left, where a professional-style grill and stove top reside, while the sink and mini-refrigerator can be found to the right of the hearth. With plenty of prep space and storage, there's no need to set foot in the kitchen on a hot summer night.

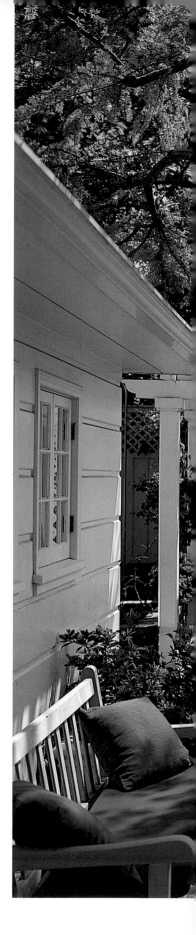

This contemporary patio proves that style and function can share the same stage. Three different levels help keep activities separate, while a minimal, modern design unifies the space. Long and somewhat narrow, the patio opens into the apartment through glass doors on the top and bottom levels. In the center is the "kitchen," separated from the other areas by two steps. One end features a table and chairs for dining along with a chaise lounge for afternoon naps. On the other side (see opposite page), comfortable chairs invite guests to sit and chat. ↺

*Built-in tiers offer both
seating and display space.*

Stainless steel moves outdoors. This sleek countertop features two burners, a sink, and abundant storage below. Though shallow, the counter is long enough to serve as an efficient staging area for meals. A small shelf mounted to the wall above the unit provides an additional utility and display surface. ➲

This house constructed of stonework is rustic, but by no means lacking in modern comforts. The open-air kitchen boasts its own sink and state-of-the-art grill (along with a rotisserie and oven). The slate countertop is a complement to the masonry of the house and provides convenient resting places for hot dishes. ○

With a little planning you can incorporate an outdoor grill—and other amenities—into the overall design of your exterior space. Housed in an attractive brick niche, this grill makes a strong architectural statement. On the practical side, it's located out of the way and has a convenient area to stow condiments or rest a plate. ➲

If your climate and space allow, a permanent outdoor kitchen is a wonderful amenity. Some shelter, counter space, wiring, and lighting are all necessary. And like a well-designed indoor kitchen, an outdoor cooking center should have adequate storage. This extended countertop, covered in ceramic tile, houses a grill and wet bar with plenty of room to rest a tray or prepare snacks. Underneath, convenient cupboards store glasses, cooking utensils—or extra beach towels. ◖

The Perfect Table

The outdoor dining table—informal, inviting, and laden with the **bounty** of the season—is often the focal point of a deck or patio. Whether you love to host huge family barbecues or plan to enjoy breezy outdoor breakfasts, this will be the place to do it. You'll want to think first about how you'll use the table, then consider the best location, and finally, the details. Will the table be large or small (but expandable)? How many chairs can it accommodate? Is there shelter from wind and sun? What kind of lighting, tableware, and other amenities do you want? The perfect setting will ensure maximum enjoyment—and **memories to savor!**

bright ideas

▶ Use a rolling serving cart with wheels to ferry food and drinks

▶ Mix and match benches and chairs (benches are ideal for kids)

▶ Invest in an expandable dining table (with leaves) for hosting larger groups

Votive candles lined up along the mantel highlight the niche above.

A sloping yard has been transformed into an outdoor room that is perfect for alfresco dining. A generous open hearth, plus walls and flooring of local stone, set the tone. The clean lines of the wood table are offset by the graceful curves of the chairs, adding a modern touch to the rustic setting. Lanterns hanging from the beams above contribute to the cozy ambience and cast a warm glow when the sun sets.

Intimate meals are a daily delight on this small private patio. A wall-mounted fountain provides soothing background music, while the majolica artwork above draws the eye toward the arched ceiling. Simple metal furniture with cushions in a classic striped fabric makes lingering over a long meal a pleasure. ◖

Don't forget to install an electrical outlet—it will come in handy for lighting, music, and more.

Sturdy columns topped by rustic wooden beams create a simple yet charming pergola to shelter a casual dining spot. Vines flourish, letting dappled sunlight filter through. The weathered garden table and chairs are a nice complement to the stone patio. A low wall behind the table further defines the space, and serves as a convenient shelf. ◑

Lavish pots of plants and a tangle of overhead vines evoke a storybook magic in this small garden. A large table would be overwhelming on such a petite patio, but a café table and folding chairs are just right. A flowery cloth sets the scene for an afternoon tea party. ↻

Four sturdy stools surround a café-height table—perfect for casual snacking and drinking. A favorite among kids, it can also serve as an overflow table when large groups gather for summer barbecues. ➲

A simple patio umbrella—available in several shapes and sizes—is all that is needed to provide a comfortable amount of shade.

Outdoor furniture that showcases its natural style is at home amid surrounding plants and trees. A rough-hewn table and bent-wood chairs lend a rustic air to this patio dining spot. The oversized garden umbrella, strung with twinkling lights, shelters the eating area during the day, while providing evening diners with a starry ceiling. ◑

Inspired by the country villas of Tuscany, a patio with a gently sloping stone wall becomes a private place to enjoy outdoor meals. White wicker chairs graced with summery cushions and billowy table linens offer a light and airy contrast to the natural stone. ☺

Outdoor Living

One of the greatest pleasures of outdoor living lies in spending time in a space that is as comfortable as an indoor room—yet it is set amid fresh air and the beauties of nature. Consider setting aside part of your deck or patio for an "outdoor room" of your own. Use trellises, arbors, canopies, or awnings to help define the boundaries of the room and provide protection from the elements. Then introduce details to create a relaxing private retreat, a reading nook, or an alcove for outdoor entertaining.

bright ideas

▶ Keep air circulating by installing a ceiling fan

▶ Install vertical shades for additional protection from the elements

▶ Bring green into an outdoor room with potted plants

An urban rooftop is transformed into a lush retreat thanks to an extensive container garden featuring plants of all sizes. Tall trees help to obscure neighboring buildings. The addition of a canopied cabana creates a private refuge with indoor comforts.

Sisal is a good choice for an outdoor room— as long as it is protected from rain.

A fireplace along one wall is framed by two substantial columns that uphold an arbor of bougainvillea and help define this alcove "reading room." Exotic elements combined with accessible furnishings—a Moroccan style occasional table and traditional wicker chairs—add a personal touch to this patio. ☻

Latticework and a simple overhead structure such as this enclose an outdoor area with minimal effort. Just add some comfortable furnishings, a few pillows, the right lighting and, before you know it, you'll be staying out all night! ☻

Outdoor rooms can be as stylish and functional as indoor ones. Tucked into a corner and protected by a white canvas awning, this covered deck shows off a collection of antique furniture, including Windsor chairs and a sizable hutch for storing and displaying dinnerware. ⮉

Here, floral fabrics are paired with wicker furnishing for a cozy, romantic look. The print featured on the sofa cushions repeats the pattern used for the tablecloth (above), tying the two areas together. The checkerboard floors are another decorative touch that enhances the traditional styling and unifies the space. ➲

Strong awning poles keep the canopy in place: consult a professional if you are planning a semi-permanent shelter.

A simple and quick way to give a sheltered, interior ambience to a deck is to drape billowy fabric across its length. Here, a pair of benches and a table await guests who'll pass a pleasant afternoon. ◖

Terra-cotta colored columns provide support for this temporary structure made of tightly gathered fabric and simple wooden beams. The canopy provides a perfect amount of shade for a circle of friends to sit comfortably on the sturdy chairs and benches while enjoying teatime snacks. ◐

Inspirations

Great spaces often result from **personal passions**. When it comes to the design of an exterior space, sources of inspiration are myriad. Your dream deck or patio may be influenced by the beauties of the landscape at hand or by visions of more **exotic** places. Favorite colors, textures, materials, and objets d'art may all influence your design perspective. Look to both your secret desires and to the world around you for ideas, and **don't limit yourself**. With inspiration, you will achieve a harmonious balance.

The beauty and strength of bamboo inspired this tropical patio. Protected from the weather by a thatched roof, the patio also has bamboo shades that can be lowered when tropical rainstorms threaten. Beneath the roof, a comfortable living room features a bamboo sofa and chaise. Simple white cotton cushions enhance the natural effect, while the tile floor adds an earthy base to the space. ➲

Artisanal stone- and brickwork give this covered patio its special character. The exquisite workmanship around the doorway and windows form the main decorative element of the patio; ceramic urns showcase local craftsmanship. The mix of materials—bamboo, clay, and stone—creates a textured look that is soothing to the body and soul. ☺

A series of Eastern-inspired patios and pools forms a harmonious whole, embodying the simplicity that is a hallmark of Zen design. Note the inset of river stones in the patio and the natural base of the column as it comes to rest in the pool. ↻

Water plants can be potted and placed into ponds for easy care and convenience.

Inspired by Chinese architecture, a pristine pavilion presides over this patio area. The water from the lily pool merges with the structure and seems to pass under it. ☊

This small deck is set within a garden pool, inviting contemplation and a reverence for nature. Perfectly integrated into this lush site, the six-sided deck incorporates an existing tree. With just enough room for two chairs, this space has a minimal impact on the natural world around it. ➲

Slabs of stone subtly mark the way to the deck. ⋂

A prime example of the splendid results that can emerge from designing with a specific site in mind, the deck that graces this home encourages visitors on a journey through the landscape. A set of winding steps flows from the deck down to a nearby stream, where a graceful bridge spans the water without disturbing the natural surroundings, and invites guests to explore the woods. ☾

Some designers might have viewed this enormous boulder as an impediment, but the designer of this space viewed it as a valuable element. The result is a simple deck that incorporates the boulder as a wall, offering the opportunity to enjoy an elegant meal in natural surroundings. Rocks and trees serve as natural barriers, ensuring privacy and a sense of calm. Sometimes it's best to follow nature's lead. ♋

Surrounded by Green

utdoor living means not only being surrounded by **natural beauty**, but also growing some of your own. Plants—be they flowers, shrubs, vines, or trees, in pots or beds—are essential elements of an appealing patio or deck. They soften the hard lines of construction and help to create a **transition** between the home and the natural environment. Another plus: for many of us, planning a garden is as enjoyable as relaxing in it.

bright ideas

- ▶ Blend integrated planters with their surroundings
- ▶ Use planters without bottoms so that roots can grow freely into the native soil
- ▶ Feature planters at different heights to add a colorful, vertical interest

This gravel patio is a mix of formal and informal elements. Symmetrical plantings border the space in green. Defining the seating area is a pair of topiaries in terra-cotta pots; their bushy tops are contrasted by the overflowing greenery planted beneath. ➲

Turning an unexpected object into a planter adds a whimsical touch to a patio. This Radio Flyer houses shrubs and a slab of slate that serves as a surface for decorative objects. ☝

An enclosed brick patio benefits from the presence of large overhanging trees; more greenery comes from a thickly planted border along the wall, and an extensive collection of potted plants. A brick patio makes an excellent surface for a potted garden. Mix and match a variety of containers, and choose plants of differing heights. ➲

This enclosed patio incorporated a large shade tree into the center of its design. A circular raised bed that also holds smaller plants and flowers was built around the base of the tree, while deep beds along the outside wall house a collection of leafy plants. ◑

A blue-tiled fountain adds vibrant color, as well as the soothing splash of water, to the patio.

Paths and entryways are ideal spots for plantings, which both highlight and soften transitions. Here, a natural stone path leads to the patio through a trellised arch, while flowers and climbers embellish the route. ♾

Chinese lanterns pick up on the colors of the flowers and add a fun, cheery touch.

Even a tiny patio can become a garden paradise. This small but charming space is festooned with flowers in brilliant colors. Climbers and potted plants are grouped to create a feeling of abundance. A bare wall becomes both useful and decorative with the addition of a small shelf with mini pots and watering cans. ☢

With a little creativity, a potted garden can add a bountiful touch to an otherwise minimalist patio. This collection is housed in containers of cast stone. ➲

Urban Oases

Some of the most bountiful **gardens** can be found hidden away on urban patios and decks, where pots and containers overflow with thriving flowers and greenery. City dwellers appreciate every square inch of outdoor space that comes their way, turning even tiny **rooftop** patches and diminutive balconies into refreshing retreats. Creating an outdoor oasis in an urban setting presents some particular challenges, including considerations of weight and watering, so professional advice may be in order. A true **passion for plants** cannot be thwarted, however, as successful city gardeners everywhere know!

bright ideas

- Purchase drought-resistant plants if your rooftop is extremely hot and dry

- Use a potting work station with plenty of storage

- Dress up inexpensive furniture with slipcovers, cushions, and flowing table linens

Miniature lights glow at sunset, a twinkling counterpart to the bright city lights.

A rooftop deck with a breathtaking skyline view is an unbeatable location for alfresco dining. Bordered by abundant planters and protected by a climber-entwined pergola, this deck offers a restorative retreat from the city below.

Long and narrow spaces can represent a challenge, but such dimensions did not deter this gardener, who transformed the patio into a flowery paradise with an abundance of potted plants. Trompe l'oeil on one garden wall extends the space visually, while plantings around the perimeter soften the structures. A small table and chairs provide a spot to sit amid the flowers. ⊂

The woven screen fencing provides privacy while letting air circulate.

A series of steps is accented with potted plants that lead the way to the top level of this urban patio. On the lower level, a small marble-topped café table and chairs with tie-on cushions provide a pleasant place to relax or read the morning paper. From the table, the view is all green—thanks to the potted garden and vines creeping up the wall. ∩

This gravel-covered courtyard has been set with wood decking in a parquet pattern to create a sitting area. An extensive container garden, accented with rounded stones, adds greenery. The effect is a peaceful hideaway, a place to keep the outside world—and worries—at bay. ↻

A retractable awning is an excellent solution for urban rooftops.

A Zen sensibility is at work here, transforming a large rooftop into a tranquil escape. Small pebbles used as flooring combine with bamboo latticework and built-in seating to create a minimal yet textured environment. Vines, trees, and evergreen shrubs provide an expanse of green that draws the eye and soothes the soul. ➲

Light Up the Night

aytime is only half the story—sunset is an event to look forward to if it means an evening spent relaxing on the deck or patio. The key to **savoring** outdoor pleasures at night is good lighting. Appropriate outdoor lighting has practical benefits (safety and security being two of them) and aesthetic appeal. Lighting can create a mood or emphasize features of the space—for instance, a spotlight can illuminate an interesting architectural detail, a garden sculpture, or a beautiful tree. When planning, consider which areas should be well lit, and where you might opt for the softer *glow* of candles or torches.

bright ideas

▶ Mount lights on stair risers as a safety measure

▶ Alternate lighted pavers with stone pavers

▶ Silhouette an ornamental tree with back lighting

Path lighting casts a soft glow on the walkways, and adds a decorative element to the deck. Placement of path lighting is important: lamps should be regularly spaced, with a height within one to two feet (15–30cm) of the ground to cast light directly on the path. ➲

The upper level of this redwood deck is surrounded by trees and has a welcome glow at night. The six-sided deck pod has finial-type lights mounted directly to the railing, providing plenty of illumination for nighttime entertaining. ⦿

The owners of this ranch house understand the importance of well-placed lighting. A bright wall sconce and recessed lighting along the overhanging roof illuminate the glass divide between interior and exterior, while spotlights set into the ground draw attention to trees, plant beds, and bench seating. ☺

plan ahead

- ☐ Custom build recessed lighting into overhead structures

- ☐ For security, install a light system regulated by a photo-cell timer, which turns on at dusk and off at dawn

- ☐ Be aware that lighting systems hooked up to household current need to be installed by a licensed electrician

Bamboo torches fitted with small votives add a tropical note to an outdoor patio. Use torches that can be stuck in the ground to create a circle of light around an entertaining area. Try insect-repelling citronella candles to keep pests away. ⊙

An assortment of candles, lanterns, and small tea lights are tucked at different levels around this patio, creating a warm and inviting atmosphere for an evening meal. ➲

A covered walkway, illuminated at night, makes a strong architectural statement against the backdrop of the rock face behind it. Floodlights were used to throw a broad wash of light upward to highlight the texture of the rock. ☉

The ceiling light on the second-floor porch creates a dramatic glow in the distance. ⋯⋯

This massive stone fireplace anchors the patio, and the warm glow of its hearth beckons guests to pull up chairs and enjoy the special pleasures of an evening spent outdoors. ➲

Grill Worksheet

Buying a grill is one of the most important purchases you'll make for your deck or patio. There are many styles available that will suit a variety of budgets—from small, 24-inch-wide drop-in units to large, ready-made cooking islands with wide grills and generous work surfaces. Before buying, consider the following to ensure that the grill you purchase suits your needs:

How large is the cooking area of the grill? Consider how many people you cook for on a regular basis, and whether or not the grill can accommodate the appropriate amount of food. If you entertain frequently, you may want a grill with a larger cooking surface to minimize the need to cook food in shifts.

Is the grill designed to accommodate the kinds of food you usually prepare? Today's grills are available with many special features from griddles to rotisseries. Think about whether you will need these features before investing in a grill chock full of extras. Buy a grill with only the features you are likely to use—it's a good way to stay within your budget.

How easy is the grill to operate and maintain? Make sure that the basic controls of the grill are accessible and easy to read. Grates should be simple to remove and adjust, and the grease pan should offer easy access for cleaning. If you are preparing to buy a grill with lots of special features, understand how each one is operated before you take your purchase home.

Review the warranty before you make a purchase. In addition to length of coverage, understand the finer points of the warranty. Note exactly what is covered; different components of the grill may be covered for different lengths of time.

Understand installation requirements. It's important to review how the grill will need to be installed, and to research any local building codes that might affect installation—such as where and how the grill can be situated. Note whether the grill is configured for natural or propane gas or both.

Look for some of these special grill features:

- Food-warming racks that can heat bread and vegetables
- Individually controlled cooking zones that provide flexibility for cooking different foods
- Rotisserie that allows you to slow-cook foods like chicken
- Griddle to expand the types of foods you can cook outdoors—think pancakes!
- Stove side-burner to allow you to prepare side dishes alongside the barbecue
- Storage bins or drawers for barbecue accessories
- Crossover ignition that lights all burners with one ignition
- Screens built into the gas ports of the burners to prevent spiders from spinning webs which block gas flow

Resources

Professional Advice

If you are interested in hiring a professional to help with the construction or remodeling of your home and outdoor space, the following associations may be helpful:

American Institute of Architects (AIA)—When making structural changes, an architect should be considered. Many, but not all, architects belong to the American Institute of Architects. Call (202) 626-7300 for information and the phone number of your local chapter. www.aiaonline.com

American Society of Interior Designers (ASID)—An interior designer can provide helpful advice especially when remodeling an existing space. The American Society of Interior Designers represents over 20,000 professionally qualified interior designers. Call ASID's client referral service at (800) 775-ASID. www.asid.org

American Society of Landscape Architects (ASLA)—Landscape architecture is the profession that encompasses the analysis planning, design, management, and stewardship of outdoor space and land. Activities of a landscape architect are varied and cover a wide range of projects including public, commercial, and residential areas. Contact ASLA by calling (202) 898-2444. Through its website, ASLA provides tips on selecting a landscape architect, and access to members of the association. www.asla.org

Associated Landscape Contractors of America (ALCA)—ALCA members are a unique blend of landscape maintenance, installation, design build contractors, and interior landscape firms. ALCA provides a list of members by region, and its website has some useful consumer tips. The ALCA phone number is (800) 395-2522. www.alca.org

National Association of the Remodeling Industry (NARI)—When it's time to select a contractor to work on your project, you might consider a member of the National Association of the Remodeling Industry. Call (800) 611-6274 for more information. www.nari.org

National Association of Home Builders (NAHB)—When you're looking at builders, it may be a good idea to contact the National Association of Home Builders. Call (800) 368-5242 for more information. www.nahb.org

OTHER RESOURCES

The following manufacturers, associations, and resources may be helpful as you plan your patio or deck.

DECKING, RAILING, FENCING

Your local lumberyard is a good place to start if you're planning to build a wood deck. They may have a list of local contractors that they recommend. Below are several other sources for information on deck and patio surfaces:

California Redwood Association (CRA)—
The California Redwood Association is the trade association for redwood lumber producers. It's an excellent resource if you're interested in constructing your deck with redwood, and offers several books and brochures for consumers. (888) 225-7339 or (888) CALREDWOOD www.calredwood.org

Cambridge Pavingstones (201) 933-5000 www.cambridgepavers.com

The Western Red Cedar Lumber Association (WRCA)—The Western Red Cedar Lumber Association is a Vancouver-based non-profit association representing twenty-three quality producers of Western Red Cedar lumber products in Washington, Oregon, Idaho, and British Columbia, Canada. The website includes interesting facts about western red cedar and its uses. (604) 684-0266 www.wrcla.org

Country Estate (800) 445-2887 www.countryestate.com

Heritage Vinyl Products (601) 726-4223 www.heritagevinyl.com

Home Depot U.S. Store Support Center (770) 433-8211 Canadian Store Support Center (800) 668-2266 www.homedepot.com

Royal Crown (800) 488-5245 www.royalcrownltd.com

Trex Company (800) BUY TREX www.trex.com

WeatherBest (800) 521-4316 www.weatherbest.lpcorp.com

PATIOS

Patio floors should be chosen with beauty and durability in mind. Many choices of natural and manufactured materials are available. Visit a local landscaper or stone dealer in your area, and consider the resources below for specific information about a surface:

The Brick Industry Association (BIA)—BIA is primarily committed to the interests of brick manufacturers and distributors, but its website has some information relevant to consumers including an idea gallery featuring brick patios. www.bia.org

Interlocking Concrete Pavement Institute (ICPI)— ICPI is an association that represents the interlocking concrete pavement industry. Their website includes information about the history and benefits of concrete pavers as well as tips for maintenance. There is also a list of certified paver manufacturers, installers, and a member directory. www.icpi.org

Italian Trade Commission
Ceramic Tile Department
499 Park Avenue
New York, NY 10022
(212) 980-1500
www.italtrade.com

Trade Commission of Spain
Ceramic Tile Department
2655 Le Jeune Road, Suite 114
Coral Gables, FL 33134
(305) 446-4387
www.tilespain.com

LIGHTING

American Lighting
Association
P.O. Box 420288
Dallas, TX 75342-0288
(800) 274-4484
www.americanlightingassoc
.com

OUTDOOR APPLIANCES AND GRILLS

Brinkmann
(800) 468-5252
www.thebrinkmanncorp.com

Broilmaster
(866) 705-2491
www.broilmaster.com

Dynamic Cooking System
(800) 433-8466
www.dcs-range.com

Dynasty
(888) 4MAYTAG
www.dynastyrange.com

Fire Magic
(800) 332-0240
www.rhpeterson.com

Lynx
(888) 289-5969

Monogram
(800) 626-2000
www.monogram.com

Phoenix Grill
(800) 332-0240
www.phoenixgrill.com

Thermador
(800) 656-9226
www.thermador.com

Ultimate Grill
(800) 626-6488
www.ultimategrill.com

Viking
(877) 834-8222
www.vikingrange.com

Weber
(888) 845-4641
www.weber.com

OUTDOOR FURNITURE AND ACCESSORIES

Country Casual
(800) 284-8325
www.countrycasual.com

Crate & Barrel
(800) 967-6696
www.crateandbarrel.com

Design Within Reach
(800) 846-0411
www.dwr.com

Frontgate
(800) 626-6488
www.frontgate.com

Gardener's Supply Co.
(800) 955-3370
www.gardeners.com

Gardeners Eden
(800) 822-1214
www.gardenerseden.com

Heltzer
(877) 561-5612
www.heltzer.com

Henry Hall Designs
(800) 767-7738
www.henryhalldesigns.com

Homecrest
(888) 346-4852
www.homecrest.com

Lands' End
(800) 963-4816
www.landsend.com

LL Bean
(800) 441-5713
www.llbean.com

Pier 1
(800) 245-4595
www.pier1.com

Plow & Hearth
(800) 494-7544
www.plowhearth.com

Robert Martin Designs
(718) 797-1183
www.robertmartindesigns
.com

Smith & Hawken
(800) 776-3336
www.smith-hawken.com

Sterling Creek
(800) 357-6171
www.sterlingcreek.com

Telescope Casual
(518) 642-1100
www.telescopecasual.com

Tidewater Workshop
(800) 666-TIDE
www.tidewaterworkshop.com

Vermont Outdoor Furniture
(800) 588-8834
www.vermontoutdoorfurniture.com

Williams Sonoma
(877) 822-1214
www.williams-sonoma.com

Wood Classics
(845) 255-7871
www.woodclassics.com

UMBRELLAS AND AWNINGS

Santa Barbara Umbrella
(800) 919-9464
www.sbumbrella.com

Somfy
(609) 395-1300
www.somfysystems.com

Sunbrella
(336) 227-6211
www.sunbrella.com

GAZEBOS AND GARDEN STRUCTURES

Dalton Pavilions
(215) 721-1492
www.daltonpavilions.com

LMT Products
(888) 570-5252
www.lmtproducts.com

Vixen Hill
(800) 423-2766
www.vixenhill.com

SUNROOMS, CONSERVATORIES, AND PATIO ENCLOSURES

Four Seasons Sunrooms
(800) FOUR SEASONS
www.four-seasons-sunrooms
.com

Hartford Conservatories
(800) 963-8700
www.hartford-con.com

Patio Enclosures
(800) 480-1966
www.patioenclosuresinc.com

PAINTS AND STAINS

Benjamin Moore
(800) 6 PAINT 6
www.benjaminmoore.com

Dutch Boy
(800) 828-5669
www.dutchboy.com

Minwax Company
(800) 523-9299
www.minwax.com

Pratt & Lambert
(800) BUY PRAT
www.prattandlambert.com

Sherwin-Williams
(800) 474-3794
www.sherwin-williams.com

POOLS AND SPAS

National Spa & Pool Institute
(NSPI) —The National Spa
& Pool Institute (NSPI)
is an international trade
association of more than
5,000 manufacturers,
distributors, retailers,
service companies, and
builders in the pool, spa,
and hot tub industry. NSPI
provides a consumer
directory of members,
which includes many
leading manufacturers,
and its website offers useful
consumer tips. Call
(800) 323-3996 for more
information.
www.nspi.org

WINDOWS AND DOORS

Andersen
(800) 426-4261
www.andersenwindows.com

Kolbe & Kolbe
(800) 955-8177
www.kolbe-kolbe.com

Loewen
(800) 245-2295
www.loewen.com

Marvin
(800) 241-9450
www.marvin.com

Morgan
(800) 877-9482
www.morgandoors.com

Pella
(800) 54 PELLA
www.pella.com

Pozzi
(800) 257-9663
www.pozzi.com

Photo Credits

Beate Works (beateworks.com):
©Grey Crawford: pp. 9, 25, 44 left,
59, 78, 79, 82–83, 110; ©Tim Street-
Porter: pp. 2 (Arch.: Steven Ehrlich),
11 (Arch.: Steven Ehrlich), 76–77, 85,
92–93, 108 (Designer: Cathleen
Spiegelman); ©**Steven Brooke:** p. 12
(Arch.: Charles Moore), 13
(Arch.: Scott Merrill), 28 top, 65
(Arch.: George Reed), 66, 67
(Courtesy of Home Magazine);
California Redwood Assn.: ©Ernest
Braun: pp. 37 top, 37 bottom, 49, 50,
51 top, 63 bottom, 64, 68 left, 70, 72,
119; ©Kim Brun: p. 81; ©James
Housel: p. 33; ©Dan Sellers: p. 118;
©Marvin Sloben: p. 32 top; ©Jessie
Walker: p. 43; ©Leslie Wright Dow:
p. 32 bottom; ©**Crandall and
Crandall:** p. 111 bottom; ©**Carlos
Domenech:** p. 73 (Designer: Luciano
Franco Alfari); ©**Elizabeth Whiting
& Assocs.:** pp. 28 bottom, 62, 75,
105 right, 115 right, 121 top; ©**Tria
Giovan:** pp. 54 bottom, 114–115;

©**Gross and Daley:** pp. 57, 93 right;
©**Kari Haavisto:** p. 80; **Houses and
Interiors:** ©Roger Brooks: pp. 34–35,
63 top, 122; ©David Copsey: p. 121
bottom; **The Interior Archive:**
©Helen Fickling: pp. 56 top, 102 left
(Garden Designer: Jason Payne),
102–103 (Garden Designer: Jason
Payne); ©Christopher Simon Sykes:
pp. 46 left, 46–47, 60–61; ©Edina
Van der Wyck: pp. 100–101, 101 right;
©Fritz von der Schulenburg: pp. 6
(Designer: Lars Bolander), 21 right
(Designer: Jed Johnson), 29 (Designer:
Jed Johnson), 96–97 (Arch.: Nico
Rensch); ©Henry Wilson: p. 116 left
(Designer: Roger Lockhart);
©**image/dennis krukowski:** pp. 56
bottom (Designer: Bunny Williams,
Inc.), 68–69 (Designer: JoAnne
Kuehner), 90–91(Designer: Vicente
Wolf Assocs., Inc.), 94 left (Designer:
Crain & Ventolo Assocs.), 94–95
(Designer: Crain & Ventolo Assocs.),
106 (Designer: Michael Formica, Inc.),

107 (Designer: Michael Formica, Inc.),
116–117 (Designer: Robert Zion
Landscape Architecture); ©**Mark
Lohman:** pp. 27 bottom, 48, 81 top,
88, 89, 97 right; ©Eric Roth: p.112–113;
©**Mark Samu:** p. 27 top; ©Claudio
Santini: p. 120 (Arch.: Frank & Frisch
Archs.); ©F&E Schmidt: p. 16 left;
©**Brad Simmons:** pp.16–17, 36
(Builder: Cedar Classics; Stylist:
Jeannie Oberholtzer), 38–39 (Arch./
Builder: Greg Staley; Landscape
Designer: Barry Wehrman; Stylist:
Cindy Martin), 39 right (Arch./Builder:
Greg Staley; Landscape Designer:
Barry Wehrman; Stylist: Cindy
Martin), 40–41 (Stylist: Jeannie
Oberholtzer), 44–45, 71 (Arch./Builder:
Greg Staley; Landscape Designer:
Barry Wehrman; Stylist: Cindy
Martin), 87 (Arch./Builder: Greg
Staley; Landscape Designer: Barry
Wehrman; Stylist: Cindy Martin),
104–105 (Arch./Builder: Greg Staley;
Landscape Designer: Barry Wehrman;

Stylist: Cindy Martin), 123 (Builder:
Don Breimhurst; Stylist: Joetta
Moulden); ©**Southern Pine Council:**
p. 51 bottom; ©**Tim Street-Porter:**
pp. 10 (Arch.: Hagy Belzberg), 14–15
(Designer: Barry Sloane), 24
(Designer/Owner: Angela Vestey), 58
(Designer: Kathleen Spiegelman), 74
(Designer: Tom Beeton), 84
(Designer: Frank Pennino), 86
(Designer: Kate Stamps), 98
(Designer: Linda Garland), 99
(Designer: Putu Suasa), 109
(Designer: Barton Myers), 111 top
(Designer: Andrew Virtue); ©**Brian
Vanden Brink:** pp. 18 (Arch.: Mark
Hutker & Assocs.), 19 (Weatherend
Estate Furniture), 20–21, 22 left
(Arch.: John Morris), 22–23, 26
(Arch.: Weston & Hewitson), 30–31
(Arch.: Pete Bethanis), 42 (Ron
Forest Fences), 52–53 (Weatherend
Estate Furniture), 54 top (Arch.:
Centerbrook Archs.), 55

Index